Let's Get Crafty with
Fabric-Felt

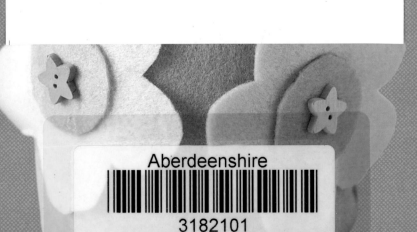

Let's Get Crafty with Fabric & Felt

FOR **KIDS AGED 2 AND UP**

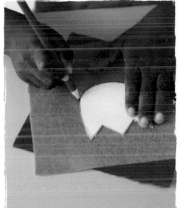

CICO **kidz**

Published in 2016 by CICO Books
An imprint of Ryland Peters & Small Ltd
20–21 Jockey's Fields   341 E 116th St
London WC1R 4BW   New York, NY 10029

www.rylandpeters.com

10 9 8 7 6 5 4 3 2 1

A CIP catalog record for this book is available from the
Library of Congress and the British Library.

ISBN: 978 1 78249 336 5

Printed in China

Editor: Katie Hardwicke
Designer: Eoghan O'Brien
Photographer: Terry Benson
Stylist: Emily Breen
Technique illustrators: Stephen Dew and
Rachel Boulton
For additional photography and styling
credits, see page 80

In-house editor: Dawn Bates
In-house designer: Fahema Khanam
Art director: Sally Powell
Head of production: Patricia Harrington
Publishing manager: Penny Craig
Publisher: Cindy Richards

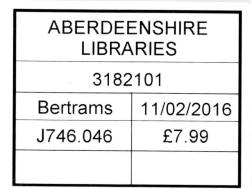

Contents

Introduction

FABRIC AND FELT ARE WONDERFUL MATERIALS FOR GETTING CRAFTY WITH YOUNG CHILDREN. EASY TO CUT AND WITH ENDLESS COLOR OPTIONS, THEY LEND THEMSELVES TO ALL TYPES OF CRAFT ACTIVITIES AND, WITH A LITTLE IMAGINATION, CAN BE TRANSFORMED INTO TOYS, GIFTS, DECORATIONS, AND ARTWORKS.

We've brought together a selection of activities that use felt and fabric, whether a sheet of felt, a fabric remnant, a T-shirt, a lonely sock, or a ball of yarn, as the starting point for getting crafty together. You'll find lots of gift ideas; the very simple and very pretty Felt Bouquet on page 34 is perfect for Mother's Day, or make a flower pot for potted plants or simply storing bits and bobs. Crafting is ideal for play date activities—the Finger Puppets on page 28 or Spoon Puppets on page 68 would keep little ones occupied with endless variations, and inspiration for jewelry fans can be found in the wonderfully simple Shoelace Necklace on page 12, or the Fabric Bangles on page 66. There are even ideas for getting messy with fabric paint, using handprints for the T-shirt on page 52, or try a little potato printing on page 32.

Cutting out, folding, gluing, wrapping, and threading are all great ways for young children to develop fine motor skills and coordination. While many projects will only need light adult supervision, there are some steps that will require your help. We have marked these with a helping hands symbol as a guide. Working as a team is all part of the fun and your child will enjoy spending time with you and learning from you, as you get crafty together.

Top Tips for Happy Crafting!

Getting crafty can mean getting messy. Follow these tips to involve your child in preparing and clearing up when crafting together:

- Cover your work table with newspaper or a wipe-down sheet or tablecloth
- Protect your child's clothes with an apron or old T-shirt (you may want to do the same!)
- Roll up sleeves and tie long hair out of the way
- Keep a roll of paper towels close by

When you've finished:

- Replace lids on glue or paint pots and felt-tipped pens
- Throw away newspaper and scraps of paper and wipe down surfaces
- Put any equipment or materials away in drawers or boxes to keep it organized and easy to find next time

WHAT YOU WILL NEED

For all the projects you will need some basic craft materials. Keep a dedicated corner or drawer for storing your equipment, and stock up on a few craft materials for the finishing touches—a good supply of googly eyes is essential!

Don't forget your fabric stash—scraps of leftover fabric, ribbons, braid, and yarn, along with buttons and beads, can all be put to good use. Many projects can also be made from recycled clothes, using fabric from outgrown dresses, tops, or pants/trousers, or transform lonely socks into fabulous creatures that will become treasured toys.

BASIC EQUIPMENT

- Ruler or tape measure
- Eraser
- White or colored construction paper
- Card for templates
- Tracing paper
- Craft scissors
- Sharp paper scissors
- Fabric scissors (do not use for cutting paper)
- Pinking shears
- Sewing and embroidery needles
- Safety pins
- Acrylic paints
- Paintbrushes
- Felt-tipped pens or marker pens
- White/PVA glue
- Glue stick

CRAFT MATERIALS

- Sheets of colored felt
- Googly eyes
- Pipe cleaners
- Pom-poms
- Cotton balls
- Glitter or sprinkles
- Sequins, sticky-backed gems
- Wooden shapes
- Elastic bands

FABRIC STASH AND RECYCLING

- Buttons, ribbons, braid, beads
- Fabric scraps or remnants
- Yarn
- Embroidery floss/thread
- Sewing thread
- Outgrown clothes
- Socks
- Plastic containers
- Cardboard boxes, egg cartons, or cereal boxes

TECHNIQUES

CUTTING OUT

Using scissors to cut a straight line is a skill that most young children can master with children's craft scissors. However, several of the projects require you to cut out detailed shapes and we have suggested that an adult help with these stages, either guiding your child or cutting out yourself. Here are a few tips to make cutting out easier and safer:

• Cutting rounded or detailed shapes: hold the scissors steady in one place and let your other hand move the paper as you cut, rather than moving the scissors.

• Cutting windows or holes: to cut out a window or hole from the center of a shape, use the point of the scissors to pierce the paper in the center of the shape, cut a slit to the inner edge, then cut out around the inner edge to remove the shape.

• Cutting circles: some projects require you to cut circles. This is quite tricky for little hands, and even big hands: keep the scissors in one place and turn the paper as you cut, or alternatively draw around a button, bobbin, or other round object first to make a template, then cut out.

• Pinking shears: use these when cutting fabrics that are likely to fray, to prevent the need for seams or hems. The zigzag line also makes a decorative edge on felt. Pinking shears are too heavy and cumbersome for small hands to use, so adult help will be required.

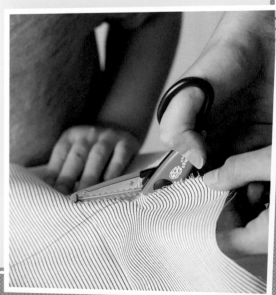

SIMPLE SEWING

Some of the projects require some basic sewing skills, and we have suggested that an adult help with these stages. We've given a brief guide to some simple stitches and sewing on buttons. With a little guidance, young children are able to sew basic stitches, and you could take the opportunity to work on these together if you like.

RUNNING STITCH

This is the simplest stitch and can be used for embroidery or for joining two pieces of fabric.

• Secure the end of the thread with a few small stitches. Bring the needle to the front then push it back down a short distance along.

• Bring the needle back up a similar distance along, in a line, and continue to form a row of equally spaced stitches.

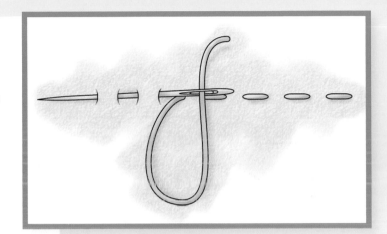

GATHERING

To gather a piece of fabric, knot your thread and begin with a few small stitches over and over in the same place to hold the thread firmly.

• Sew a line of running stitches—the smaller the stitches, the smaller the gathers you will make.

• At the end, don't finish off; leave the thread loose. Hold the thread and pull the fabric back along the line of stitches so it gathers up into folds.

• When the gathered fabric is the right width, secure the end of the thread with a few stitches over and over, then trim the thread.

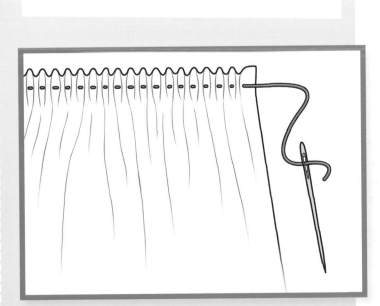

SEWING BUTTONS

• Secure the thread in the fabric with a few small stitches. Hold the button in place and bring the needle up through one of the holes in the button.

• Take the needle back down through the second hole and push through the fabric. Bring the needle back through the first hole. Repeat five or six times.

• If there are four holes in the button, use all four to make a cross pattern. Finish with a few stitches on the back.

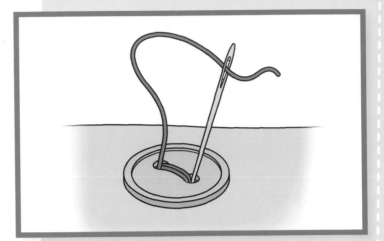

OVERSEW STITCH/WHIPSTITCH

This simple stitch is used to sew the edges of two layers of fabric or felt together, or to close up a gap after stuffing an object; it is a very simple first stitch for children to master.

• Begin with a knot or a few small stitches, either between the two layers or on the back.

• Push the needle through both layers to the front, a little way below the edge, and pull the thread through. Take the needle over the top to the back again and push it through to the front a little way along.

• Keep making stitches over and over the edges of the two fabrics. Finish with a knot or a few small stitches.

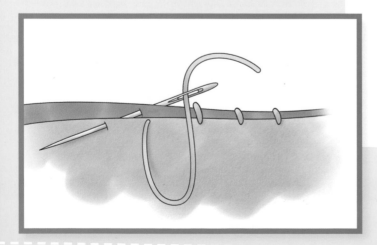

MAKING TEMPLATES

For some projects you need to transfer the template shape given on pages 74–79 onto card, before using it to cut out the final shape from the material used in the project. Use a photocopier to enlarge or reduce the shape if required, following the percentage given with the template.

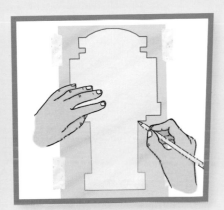

1 Once the template is the right size, place a sheet of tracing paper over the template outline and hold in place with masking tape. Trace over the lines with a hard pencil.

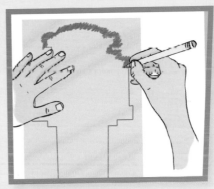

2 Turn the tracing paper over so that the back is facing you and neatly scribble over the lines with a softer pencil. Make sure all the lines are covered.

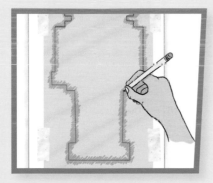

3 Turn the tracing paper over again so that the top is facing you and position it on your card, using masking tape to hold it in place. Carefully draw over the lines you made in Step 1 with the hard pencil, then remove the tracing paper. The outline will be transferred to the card. Cut out the card template to use for your project.

4 Alternatively, you can photocopy the template directly onto thin card and cut out.

USING TEMPLATES

You may need to help your child when drawing around a template:

- Hold the template in place firmly
- Use a pencil or marker pen to draw around the edge of the template onto the fabric or felt used in the project
- Keep the pencil upright and draw a steady, continuous line
- Use a white pencil on dark fabric or felt so that the outline will show clearly
- On felt, a fine-tipped marker or felt-tipped pen may be easier to see

Simple Shoelace Necklace

THREADING BEADS IS AN ACTIVITY THAT YOUNG CHILDREN CAN ENJOY UNAIDED. THE PLASTIC COATED ENDS OF SHOELACES ARE PERFECT FOR THREADING—LOOK OUT FOR PATTERNED SHOELACES THAT CAN BE TRANSFORMED INTO A GROOVY PIECE OF JEWELRY.

WHAT YOU WILL NEED

- Patterned or brightly colored shoelace
- About 20 plastic pony beads

1

THREAD THE BEADS Lay your shoelace on a flat work surface and begin to thread on your beads. Experiment with the arrangement, grouping beads together and leaving a bit of space between the groups so the pattern of the shoelace shows through.

TIE THE SHOELACE When you have threaded on all your beads, tie the ends of the shoelace together in a bow around your child's neck.

MAKE A BRACELET If you want, you can make a bracelet from the shoelace by wrapping it around your child's wrist and tying in a knot to secure it.

Sock Caterpillar

MOST HOUSEHOLDS HAVE A FEW LONELY SOCKS THAT HAVE LOST THEIR PARTNERS ALONG THE WAY. PUT THEM TO GOOD USE IN THIS FUN, NO-SEW ACTIVITY AND CREATE A CUTE TOY WITH JUST A FEW CRAFT ACCESSORIES AND A LITTLE BIT OF IMAGINATION.

WHAT YOU WILL NEED

- Clean long sock without any holes
- Cotton balls
- Elastic bands
- Colored pipe cleaner
- Scissors
- White/PVA glue
- Googly eyes

1

STUFF THE SOCK Fill the sock with cotton balls, making sure you push them all the way down to the end—you could use the end of a paintbrush to help push them down.

TIE THE HEAD Place one elastic band over the toe end of the sock and twist it in place to prevent the cotton balls from falling out.

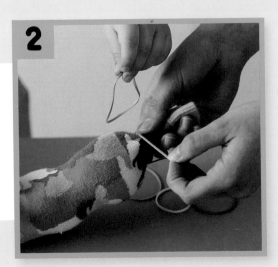

2

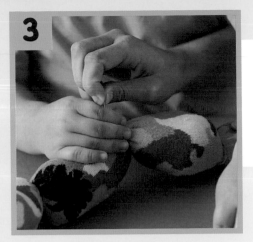

3

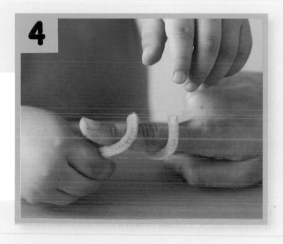

4

WRAP THE BODY Take another three or four elastic bands and twist them around the sock at regular intervals to make the sections of the body.

MAKE ANTENNAE Cut the pipe cleaner into two lengths. Wrap the pipe-cleaner pieces around your finger to make the curly ends.

5

GLUE FACE Put two dabs of glue on top of the caterpillar's head, stick the pipe cleaners in place, and then glue on the googly eyes.

Fleece Scarf

FLEECE IS A WONDERFUL FABRIC FOR FIRST-TIME CRAFTERS AS IT DOESN'T FRAY, SO THERE'S NO NEED FOR HEMMING OR SEWING. HERE, A STRIP OF FLEECE IS INSTANTLY TRANSFORMED INTO A SCARF WITH A LITTLE SNIPPING, CUTTING, AND GLUING.

WHAT YOU WILL NEED

- 8in x 1yd (20cm x 1m) piece of fleece fabric
- Fabric scissors
- Templates on page 77
- Card for template
- Pencil and scissors
- Squares of colored felt for flowers
- Scraps of colored felt for flower centers
- Fabric glue
- Decorative buttons (about ¾in/2cm diameter)

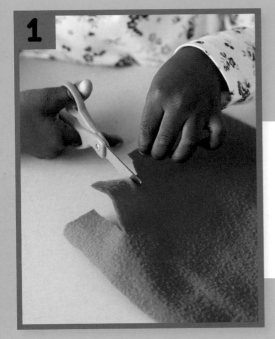

CUT A FRINGE Take the piece of fleece and, along the two short ends, cut slits about ¾in (2cm) apart and about 3in (8cm) long to create the fringing; young children may need some help cutting.

TRACE TEMPLATE Copy the flower and circle templates on page 77 onto card and cut out. Place the flower template on the felt and trace around it. Trace two flowers and two circles, all on different colored felts.

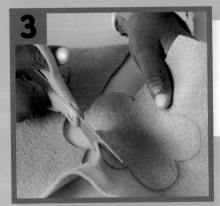

3

CUT SHAPES Cut out the felt flowers and circles; turn the felt rather than the scissors on curved shapes.

4

FINISH FLOWERS Put a dab of glue on the back of the flowers and stick them to the end of the scarf, above the fringing. Glue a circle to the center of the flowers.

5

ADD BUTTONS If you like, you can stick decorative buttons or other embellishments to the flower centers.

Funky Felt Beads

THESE BRIGHT AND COLORFUL BEADS ARE GREAT FUN TO MAKE, INVOLVING GLUING, ROLLING, AND THREADING. ASPIRING JEWELRY DESIGNERS WILL ENJOY MIXING UP THE COLORS AND CHOOSING DIFFERENT COMBINATIONS FOR NECKLACES, BRACELETS, AND HAIR ACCESSORIES.

WHAT YOU WILL NEED

- Sheets of felt in assorted colors
- Scissors
- Ruler
- White/PVA glue
- Elastic bands
- Needle and embroidery floss/thread

CUT FELT Cut out a rectangle of felt, measuring 5 x 4in (12 x 10cm). Cut a slightly smaller rectangle in another color, measuring 5 x 3in (12 x 8cm).

ADD GLUE Lay the smaller rectangle on top of the larger one, matching the 5in (12cm) width and leaving a small gap at both ends. Apply a line of glue along one exposed edge.

3

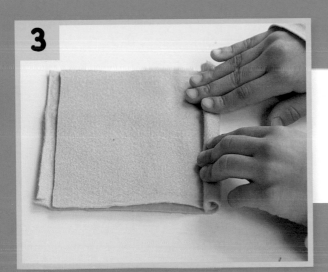

ROLL FELT Starting with the glued edge, roll up the felt into a long sausage shape.

4

GLUE FELT ROLL Put a line of glue along the remaining edge and stick the roll together, holding it in place until the glue dries with elastic bands.

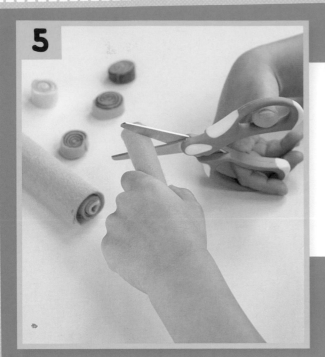

5

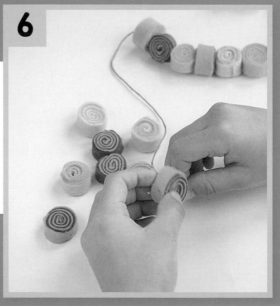

6

CUT BEADS When the glue is completely dry, use scissors to cut the felt roll into beads, making each one about ¾in (2cm) wide. Repeat these steps with different colored felts to make a selection of colorful beads.

THREAD BEADS Use a needle and embroidery floss/thread to thread the beads together to make a necklace. Try not to put beads of the same color next to each other. Tie the floss into a knot to finish.

Crafty Tip

These cute beads would look great attached to a hair barette, too—follow the instructions on page 44.

Shoebox Jewelry Box

IT'S NOT LONG BEFORE LITTLE ONES ACQUIRE A SURPRISINGLY LARGE COLLECTION OF JEWELRY. THIS CLEVER BOX, MADE FROM A RECYCLED SHOEBOX, WILL HELP TO KEEP NECKLACES FROM GETTING TANGLED, AND PROVIDE THE PERFECT SHOWCASE TO DISPLAY THEM ON A DRESSING TABLE WHEN NOT BEING WORN.

WHAT YOU WILL NEED

- Cardboard shoebox
- Colorful gift wrap and tissue paper
- Scissors
- White/PVA glue or sticky tape
- Ruler and pencil
- Ribbon
- Templates on page 76
- Card for templates
- Scraps of fabric or felt, buttons and beads, to decorate

COVER THE BOX Remove the lid from your box and cover the outside in colorful gift wrap, folding it around and gluing inside, or sticking down with sticky tape.

COVER THE INSIDE If the inside of your box is a solid color you won't need to cover it but if there are any words or designs you should cover them with paper. Use brightly colored tissue paper to contrast with the outside.

3

MEASURE THE BOX Turn the box over. Using a ruler and pencil, measure and mark 1in (2.5cm) in and 1in (2.5cm) down from the left corner of the box, then repeat at the right corner of the box. Use scissors to poke a hole on the right and left sides of the box where you marked. Be sure to poke through the card and the gift wrap on the back.

4

THREAD THE RIBBON Cut a piece of ribbon longer than the length of the box (or the width if you are going to stand your box vertically) and thread it through the hole on the left into the inside of the box (you can use the end of a pencil to guide it through). Tie a double knot on the outside of the box so the knot doesn't slip through the hole. Take the other end of the ribbon and thread it out through the right hole and tie a double knot on the outside of the box. Trim off any extra ribbon.

5

TRACE TEMPLATES Copy the templates on page 76 and cut out from card. Trace around the templates on scraps of fabric or felt and cut out.

DECORATE SHAPES Glue some pretty buttons or shapes onto your fabric pieces and let them dry.

6

7

FINISH THE BOX Glue the shapes to your box and when they are dry, you are ready to hang your necklaces from the ribbon.

Pom-pom Bee

POM-POMS ARE GREAT FUN TO MAKE, AND QUITE ADDICTIVE! YOU CAN TRANSFORM THEM INTO ALL SORTS OF BUGS AND CREATURES—TRY GLUING SEVERAL GREEN POM-POMS TOGETHER FOR A CATERPILLAR, OR MAKE A LADYBUG WITH BLACK FELT SPOTS. HERE, WE'VE MADE A CUTE BEE WITH JUST A SINGLE POM-POM, SOME FELT, AND GOOGLY EYES.

WHAT YOU WILL NEED

- Card for pom-pom and template
- Pencil and scissors
- Pom-pom maker (optional)
- Yellow yarn/wool
- Black and blue felt
- White/PVA glue
- Template on page 78
- Googly eyes
- Black craft pom-poms

1

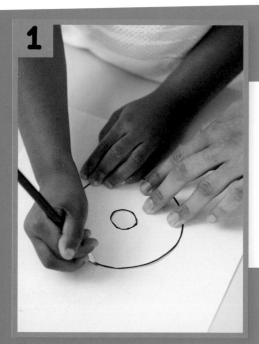

MAKE POM-POM RING Draw a circle with a diameter of 3in (8cm) on card, with a smaller 1in (2.5cm) circle in the center. Cut out around the outer circle and then cut the inner circle to make a hole. Trace around the card ring to cut out a second ring. Alternatively, use a pom-pom maker.

2

WIND YARN Put the two card circles together and start to wind the yarn around them, pulling it tightly through the hole in the middle.

Crafty Tip

We've used craft pom-poms for the antennae, but you could cut out black felt circles instead.

MAKE POM-POM Continue to wind the yarn around the card ring. To make a really dense pom-pom, keep winding the yarn over itself until the center hole is full. You may need to thread the yarn onto a darning needle to push it through the hole.

3

4

RELEASE POM-POM With a pair of scissors, carefully cut around the edge of the circle of wool, pushing the blade of the scissors between the two card discs. Cut all the way around.

5

TIE POM-POM Pull a double length of yarn between the card discs and tie it tightly with a knot, leaving a long tail.

FLUFF UP POM-POM Remove the card discs and fluff up the pom-pom. You can trim any ends of yarn if you like, to make a neat shape.

6

7

ADD BEE BODY Cut a strip of black felt, about 1in (2.5cm) wide and long enough to wrap around the pom-pom. Add a dab of glue to one end of the strip, wrap it around the middle of the pom-pom, and glue the ends together.

8

MAKE WINGS Copy the wing template on page 78 onto card, cut it out, and trace around it on blue felt. Cut out two wings. Insert the wings under the black felt strip and add a dab of glue to secure them in place.

9

FINISH BEE Glue the googly eyes to the front of the body and add two black craft pom-poms above them, for antennae. Your bee is ready to fly!

Finger Puppets

ONCE ALL THE PIECES ARE PREPARED, YOUR CHILD WILL LOVE BEING INVOLVED IN GLUING AND DESIGNING THEIR OWN FINGER PUPPETS. WE'VE GIVEN YOU TEMPLATES FOR A LION AND SHEEP, BUT YOU COULD DESIGN YOUR OWN OR CREATE CHARACTERS FROM YOUR CHILD'S FAVORITE STORIES.

WHAT YOU WILL NEED

- Templates on page 74
- Card for templates
- Pencil and scissors
- Pieces of felt in assorted colors
- Pinking shears
- White/PVA glue
- 3-D fabric paint pens

1

PREPARE Copy the templates on page 74 onto card then cut out the shapes from felt. Cut two body shapes per puppet—we used pinking shears to make a patterned edge, but normal scissors will do, as felt does not fray.

2

GLUE BODY Apply a line of glue around the edge of one body shape, leaving the bottom of the shape clear, then stick the other body shape on top. For the sheep, fold each ear in half and position at the top of the body shape before sticking the other body shape on top.

3

ADD FACE For the lion, put dots of glue on the back of the mane and carefully position it on the front of the finger puppet body. Push down firmly, then let it dry completely. Glue the sheep's face to the front of the body.

4

ADD EYES Use the 3-D fabric paint pen to draw the eyes and nose on the lion's face. Let it dry completely before playing. Do the same for the sheep.

Crafty Tip

It's easy to create finger puppet people—use felt and fabric for their clothes, and scraps of yarn for their hair.

Big Flower Brooch

YOUNG CHILDREN WILL LOVE THE CHANCE TO DESIGN THEIR OWN BROOCH USING SCRAPS OF PRETTY FABRIC AND FELT. THE FINISHED PIECE WOULD MAKE A LOVELY GIFT OR A FUN ACTIVITY FOR A PLAY DATE.

WHAT YOU WILL NEED

- Templates on page 74
- Card for templates
- Pencil and scissors
- 2 sheets of felt in different colors
- 2 squares of patterned cotton fabric
- White/PVA or fabric glue
- 1 large button
- Brooch pin

CUT OUT TEMPLATES
Copy the five flower templates on page 30 and carefully cut them out with scissors. Place the smallest flower template onto a sheet of felt and draw around it with a pencil, then cut out the shape.

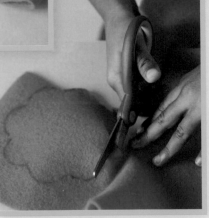

MAKE FLOWERS Lay the template for the second-smallest flower on a piece of fabric, draw around it in pencil, and cut it out. Continue drawing and cutting the flowers in size order, alternating between the felt and fabric, until you have all five.

3

GLUE THE FLOWER Starting with the largest flower at the bottom, glue the flower shapes on top of each other in size order to make a layered effect. Glue a button to the center of the smallest flower.

4

ADD BROOCH BACK To complete the brooch, stick the brooch pin to the back of the flower with a dab of glue. Let it dry completely before wearing.

Crafty Tip

Your brooch will look great on clothes, or use it to add a decorative finish to your favorite bag.

Potato Print T-shirts

THE IDEA OF COVERING VEGETABLES AND FRUIT WITH PAINT AND THEN PRINTING WITH THEM IS SURE TO APPEAL TO YOUNG CHILDREN. THE TRADITIONAL TECHNIQUE OF POTATO PRINTING CAN BE USED FOR ALL KINDS OF SHAPES AND APPLIED TO MANY SURFACES, FROM T-SHIRTS TO PAPER AND GIFT WRAP.

WHAT YOU WILL NEED

- Potatoes
- Cookie cutters
- Sharp knife
- Paper towels
- Fabric paint
- Paper plates
- Plain cotton T-shirt
- Piece of card or cardboard (a cereal packet will do)
- Buttons and ribbon, to decorate (optional)

1

PREPARE POTATO Cut a potato in half and push a cookie cutter into the cut side. Cut the potato away around the cutter, to a depth of about ½in (1cm), then remove the cutter. Dry the surface of the potato with a paper towel.

DIP IN PAINT Put some fabric paint onto a plate and dip the potato shape into it, making sure you only coat the shape. Press it lightly onto scrap paper to remove any excess paint.

2

PRINT ON T-SHIRT Insert a piece of card inside the T-shirt, to prevent the paint from seeping through. Make sure the T-shirt is smooth and crease-free, then press the potato onto the fabric, in the center, pressing firmly. Remove the potato by lifting straight up and off, so that the paint doesn't smudge.

4 **MAKE MORE PRINTS** Remove any remaining paint from the potato, then repeat the process using different colors of fabric paint.

ADD A STALK Using the other half of the potato, cut a stalk shape. Dip the stalk in green paint and print stalks onto the T-shirt. Let the paint dry thoroughly.

6  **IRON** Follow the manufacturer's instructions on the fabric paint and iron the T-shirt (if necessary) to fix the paint. For a pretty finish, sew buttons to the flower centers and a small ribbon at the base of the flower stalks.

Crafty Tip

For an apple print, cut an apple in half and dip the cut side in the paint, then print on the T-shirt. Make a leaf and stalk shapes from a potato.

Felt Bouquet

THESE SIMPLE TULIPS ARE SO EASY TO MAKE, YET THE RESULTS ARE SO PRETTY. THESE WOULD MAKE A LOVELY MOTHER'S DAY PRESENT, OR JUST TO DECORATE YOUR CHILD'S ROOM.

WHAT YOU WILL NEED

- Template on page 76
- Card for template
- Pencil and scissors
- 1 piece of red felt
- 1 piece of pink felt
- 1 piece of green felt
- 8 pipe cleaners
- Sheet of construction paper (optional)

MAKE TEMPLATES Copy the leaf and tulip templates on page 34 onto card. Draw around your templates on the pieces of felt until you have two red flowers, two pink flowers, and four green leaves. Cut them out.

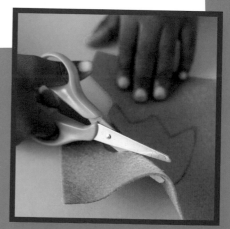

SNIP FLOWERS Bend your flowers in half from side to side and make two tiny ¼-in (5-mm) snips ¾in (2cm) from the top and bottom. Repeat this with the leaves.

ADD STEMS Feed your pipe cleaners through the holes in the felt flowers and leaves to make the flower stems.

Crafty Tip

Gather all your flowers and leaves together and wrap them in a cone of paper to make a bouquet, if you like.

Ribbon and Bow Necklace

RIBBONS ARE AVAILABLE IN SO MANY PRETTY PATTERNS AND COLORS. THEY ARE THE PERFECT BASE FOR THIS NECKLACE, DECORATED WITH LITTLE FELT BOWS AND FINISHED WITH BEADS.

WHAT YOU WILL NEED

- 2 sheets of felt in different colors
- Ruler
- Scissors
- 5 beads
- White/PVA glue
- 24in (60cm) satin ribbon (1in/2.5cm wide)

1

CUT OUT BOWS From each sheet of felt, cut a strip approximately 2in (5cm) wide. From the strip, cut a piece 1in (2.5cm) wide, to give you a rectangle 1 x 2in (2.5 x 5cm). Cut two rectangles in one color, and three in the second color.

MAKE A BOW Fold the rectangle in half and cut out a triangle from the middle—this will create a bow shape when flattened out. Make five bows in this way.

2

3

GLUE ON BOWS Take your length of ribbon and fold it into a "V" shape in the middle (this will help your necklace sit flat when you wear it). Glue a bow onto the ribbon at this point to mark the center of the necklace. Continue gluing on the bows, adding two on either side.

4

ADD BEADS Glue a bead to the center of each felt bow and let dry completely before wearing.

5 **TIE IN PLACE** Tie the two ends of ribbon together in a bow around your child's neck to complete the necklace.

Fuzzy Dino Badge

DINOSAURS APPEAL TO ALL AGES, ESPECIALLY CUTE FUZZY ONES! THIS IS THE PERFECT ACTIVITY TO KEEP LITTLE ONES BUSY AT A DINOSAUR-THEMED PARTY, AND THEY CAN TAKE THEIR BADGE HOME WITH THEM AFTERWARD.

WHAT YOU WILL NEED

- White/PVA glue
- Sheet of colored card
- Sheet of felt
- Template on page 76
- Card for template
- Pencil and scissors
- Small scraps of felt in 2 different colors
- 1 googly eye
- Brooch pin

GLUE ON FELT Apply a generous amount of glue to the piece of card and then place the sheet of felt on top, smoothing it down with your hands to make sure there aren't any bubbles. Let it dry for a few minutes.

TRACE DINOSAUR Copy the dinosaur template on page 76. Cut it out and place it on top of the felt. Draw around it with a pencil or marker pen, using your other hand to hold the template in place.

CUT OUT Carefully cut out the dinosaur shape with scissors; turn the card not the scissors on the curved edges.

ADD THE SPOTS Take the scraps of felt and cut out small circles, about ¼in (5mm) in diameter. You will need four or five of each color. Use small dabs of glue to stick the spots on the dinosaur.

5

 **ADD EYE** Put a dab of glue on the head of the dinosaur and stick on the googly eye.

6

ATTACH BROOCH PIN Glue the brooch pin onto the back of the dinosaur with a dab of glue. Let it dry completely before wearing.

Under the Sea Notebook

ALL ASPIRING ARTISTS NEED A NOTEBOOK AND WHAT BETTER WAY TO PERSONALIZE IT THAN WITH A DECORATED COVER? MADE FROM SOFT FELT, WE'VE DECORATED OUR COVER WITH A SEA LIFE THEME, BUT YOU CAN ADAPT THE IDEA FOR ANY SHAPES.

WHAT YOU WILL NEED

- Hardback notebook
- Tape measure
- Pencil and scissors
- Large sheet of felt for cover
- Safety pins
- Templates on page 78
- Card for templates
- Scraps of colored felt for jellyfish, fish, and starfish
- Blue yarn
- White/PVA glue
- Googly eyes
- Black marker pen
- Stranded embroidery floss/thread and needle

MEASURE COVER With the notebook open and flat, use a tape measure to measure the outside cover. Add ½in (1cm) to the height and 6in (15cm) to the width—to create a 3in (8cm) flap at each end. Draw the measurements directly onto the back of a sheet of felt, and cut out the rectangle.

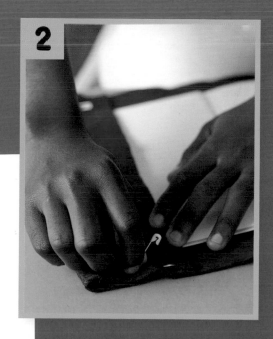

MAKE THE FLAPS Wrap the piece of felt around the book, with the front ends folded over inside the book's cover by 3in (8cm) at each end. Crease the folds and pin in place with a safety pin to hold the cover in place while you decorate it. Check that you can open and close the book easily.

3

MAKE TEMPLATES Copy the templates on page 78 and cut out. Trace around the shapes on different colors of felt and cut out a jellyfish, a starfish, and two small fish.

MAKE JELLYFISH Cut five lengths of yarn, about 2½in (6cm) long. Position the strands on the back of the jellyfish on the scalloped edge and glue in place.

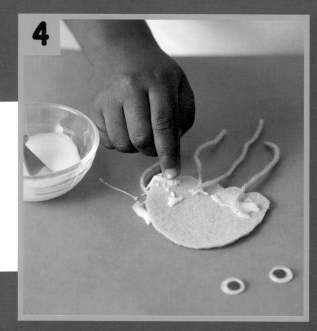

4

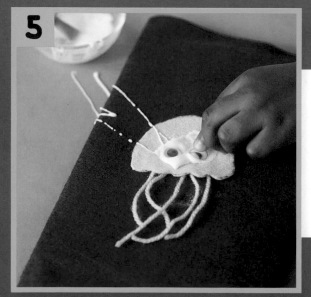

5

ATTACH JELLYFISH Next, glue the jellyfish on the felt notebook cover, with the yarn legs dangling down. Glue some googly eyes onto your jellyfish!

6

ADD FISH Glue the fish onto the cover and use a black marker pen to add eyes. Glue the starfish to the back cover and then let everything dry completely.

SEW TOGETHER Remove the book from the cover. Use embroidery floss/thread and large running stitches to sew along the top and bottom of the cover, taking a ¼in (5mm) seam. Sew through both layers of the flap to secure the cover in place. Remove the safety pins.

7

Button Barrette

THIS IS A GREAT INTRODUCTION TO JEWELRY MAKING AND WILL APPEAL TO ALL THOSE WHO LOVE TO ACCESSORIZE! YOU CAN USE ALL SORTS OF CRAFT OR SEWING EMBELLISHMENTS, AND IT'S A GREAT CHANCE TO PUT TO GOOD USE ALL THE BITS AND BOBS THAT HAVE GATHERED AT THE BOTTOM OF YOUR SEWING STASH.

WHAT YOU WILL NEED

- Plain hair barrette
- Glue stick
- Sheet of colored felt
- Scissors
- Assorted buttons
- White/PVA glue

1

APPLY THE GLUE Hold the underside of the hair barrette in one hand and use the other hand to apply glue to the flat surface of the barrette with the glue stick. You will need quite a thick layer.

STICK ON THE FELT Press the felt onto the glued surface of the hair barrette and let it dry. When dry, use scissors to cut around the barrette shape.

2

3

ADD BUTTONS Decide the order for your buttons, laying them out on a flat work surface. Starting from one end, apply a dab of glue to the felt surface and stick on the first button. Continue to apply glue and buttons along the length of the hair barrette. Let it dry completely before wearing.

Variation

You could replace the buttons with fun embellishments like craft pom-poms, wooden shapes, or sticky-backed gems.

Cotton Ball Sheep

THIS CUTE, FLUFFY CHARACTER IS EASILY MADE FROM A FEW SIMPLE MATERIALS, WITH LOTS OF GLUING FUN ALONG THE WAY. ONCE YOU'VE NAMED YOUR SHEEP, HE'LL BE THE PERFECT TOY FOR IMAGINATIVE PLAY OR STORYTIME.

WHAT YOU WILL NEED

- Paper or plastic cup (or recycle a clean, small yogurt container)
- White/PVA glue
- Cotton balls
- Template on page 79
- Card for template
- Pencil and scissors
- Sheet of black felt

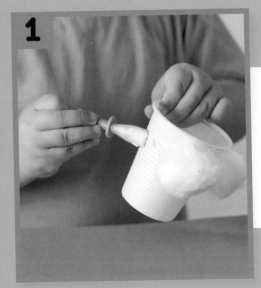

1

ADD GLUE Add a line of glue around the top of the cup and one by one, stick cotton balls along the glue line.

COVER CUP Continue adding glue and cotton balls around the cup until the entire cup (including the base) is covered in cotton balls.

2

3

4

TRACE FACE Copy the template on page 79 and cut out. Trace around the circle onto the black felt, using a white pencil so that you can see the line. Cut out the circle.

ADD EYES Stick the googly eyes to the top of the felt circle, then stick the circle to the cotton ball cup.

5

ADD EARS Cut out two small oval shapes from the black felt for ears. Glue the sheep's ears onto the body, above the face.

Cat Mask

FELINE FANS WILL ADORE THIS MASK—IT'S PERFECT FOR PLAYTIME OR FANCY DRESS PARTIES, AND CAN EASILY BE ADAPTED INTO A BLACK CAT FOR HALLOWEEN.

WHAT YOU WILL NEED

- Templates on page 77
- Card for templates
- Pencil and scissors
- Sheets of brown, black, and cream felt
- Black craft pom-pom
- Orange, brown, and black pipe cleaners
- White/PVA glue
- Hole punch
- Elastic thread

MAKE TEMPLATES Copy the face template on page 77 onto a piece of folded card and cut out. Check that it's the right size for your face and adjust if necessary. Open out the template to give you the whole shape. Glue the face shape onto the brown felt and let it dry.

CUT OUT MASK Carefully cut out around the card shape. To cut the eye holes, make a slit in the card in the center of the eyes so that the point of the scissors can be inserted.

3

MAKE FACIAL FEATURES Copy the remaining templates on page 77 onto card and cut out. For the cat's stripes, trace around the small triangle on the edge of the cream felt twice, trace around the larger triangle once, and cut out all three. Trace around the ear template twice onto black felt and cut out. Finally trace around the mouth template onto cream felt and cut out.

ATTACH WHISKERS AND FEATURES Cut six pipe-cleaner whiskers measuring approximately 4in (10cm) long, and glue three to each side of the mask, just below the eye holes. Glue the mouth, pom-pom nose, and other features onto the mask. Let it dry completely.

4

5

THREAD ELASTIC Using a hole punch, make a hole on each side of the mask as indicated on the template. Thread one end of the elastic through the hole and knot to secure. Thread the elastic through the other hole, check the fit, then knot and trim any elastic to finish.

Sock Puppet

HAND PUPPETS MAKE PERFECT PLAYTIME COMPANIONS. THIS ONE IS EASILY MADE FROM A SOCK WITH THE ADDITION OF A COUPLE OF BUTTON EYES AND A CRAZY MOP OF HAIR— IT WILL SOON BE JOINING IN AT STORYTIME!

WHAT YOU WILL NEED

- Clean long sock
- Marker pen
- Templates on page 74
- Card for templates
- Pencil and scissors
- Felt (any color)
- White/PVA glue
- 2 buttons
- Yarn/wool

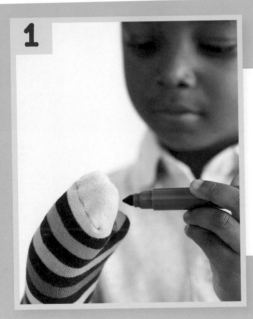

1

MARK THE EYES AND MOUTH Put your hand inside the sock so that your fingertips are at the tip of the toe portion of the sock. Using a marker pen, mark dots on the underside for the mouth, and on the top for where you would like to place the eyes, then remove your hand from the sock.

CUT OUT FELT EYES AND MOUTH Copy the templates on page 74 onto card and cut out. Trace around the templates onto your felt to make two eyes and one mouth. Cut out.

2

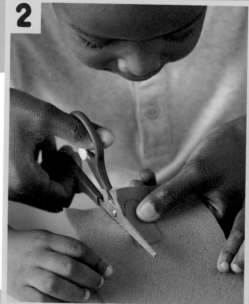

GLUE MOUTH Glue the mouth where you made a mark on the underside of the sock.

GLUE EYES Now put dabs of glue where you marked the eyes and stick the felt circles in place. Allow to dry, then glue a button on top of each circle of felt.

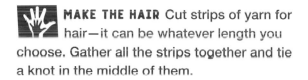 **MAKE THE HAIR** Cut strips of yarn for hair—it can be whatever length you choose. Gather all the strips together and tie a knot in the middle of them.

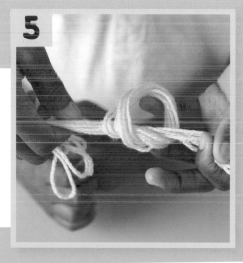

STICK THE HAIR ON Put your hand inside the sock to have a look at your Sock Puppet and decide where to position the hair. Place a dab of glue on the top of the head and press the knot in the yarn firmly in place. Let it dry before playing!

Handprint T-shirt

TIME TO GET MESSY! HANDPRINTS ARE GREAT FUN AND WHEN APPLIED WITH FABRIC PAINT, YOU'LL HAVE A MEMORABLE RECORD OF YOUR CHILD'S LITTLE HANDS IN A PERSONALIZED ARTWORK THAT THEY'LL LOVE TO WEAR.

WHAT YOU WILL NEED

- Plain cotton T-shirt
- Sheet of card or cardboard (a cereal packet would work)
- Fabric paints in different colors
- Paintbrush

1

PREPARE To prevent the paint from seeping through to the back of the T-shirt, insert a piece of card or cardboard inside the T-shirt. Make sure the fabric is smooth and flat, with no creases, before you start to print.

PAINT HAND Use the paintbrush to apply a generous amount of paint to the palm of your child's hand. Make sure that their fingers are spread.

2

3

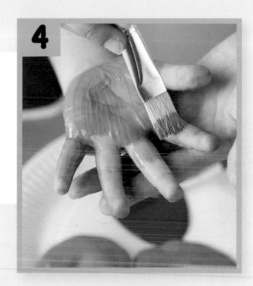

4

MAKE HANDPRINT To prevent smudges, hold your child's arm and guide their hand flat onto the fabric. Hold and press briefly, then lift the hand straight up and off to leave a clean print.

ADD MORE PRINTS Wash and dry your child's hand and then repeat with the opposite hand and different colors until you are happy with the design. Let dry.

5 **FINISH** Follow the fabric paint manufacturer's instructions to set the paint before wearing or washing the T-shirt.

Spring Flower Pot

THIS IDEA IS LOVELY FOR A SPRINGTIME GIFT, FOR MOTHER'S DAY, OR A THANK YOU FOR GRANNY. YOU CAN CHANGE THE COLORS FOR OTHER HOLIDAYS, TOO, PERHAPS PINK WITH RED HEARTS FOR VALENTINE'S DAY, OR RED WITH WHITE SNOWFLAKES FOR CHRISTMAS.

WHAT YOU WILL NEED

- Double-sided tape
- Scissors
- Large 2-cup (500-ml) plastic container (recycle a clean plastic yogurt container)
- Large sheet of felt (good colors for spring are green, blue, pink, purple) or 2 sheets stuck together, depending on the size of your pot
- White/PVA glue
- Colored felt for flowers
- Template on page 77
- Card for template
- Shaped buttons, to decorate

PREPARE Cut six strips of double-sided tape, each one the height of the plastic container. Stick the double-sided tape, in vertical strips, around the plastic container.

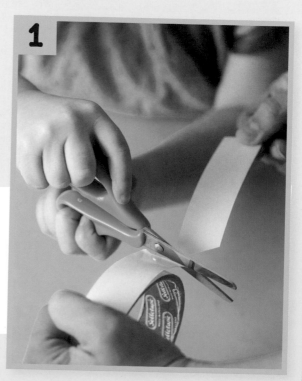

STICK ON FELT Put your taped plastic container in the middle of the piece of felt and wrap the fabric around, sticking it in place, leaving a wide border of felt at the top and bottom.

GLUE ENDS IN PLACE Apply a generous line of glue along one end of the felt and stick it down, overlapping the other end.

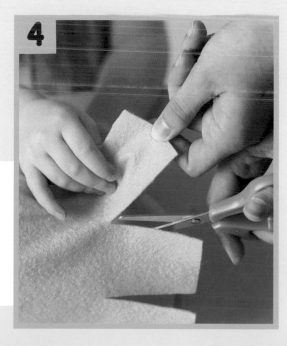

CUT SLITS Using scissors, cut wide slits from the bottom of the felt up to the base of the plastic container. Make a few slits, evenly spaced, around the base.

STICK THE BASE Add a layer of glue to the base of the plastic container and fold down and press the bottom strips of fabric into the glue so that the felt will be secured to the base of the plastic container.

STICK THE TOP Now add a line of glue along the inside top of the plastic container and along the top of the felt. Fold the felt over the top edge and press it onto the glue inside the plastic container.

MAKE TEMPLATES Copy the flower templates on page 77, cut out, and trace around them on pieces of colored felt. Cut out enough flowers and centers to go around your pot.

8

DECORATE Now it's time to decorate! Glue your flowers to the pot and add little shaped buttons to the centers.

Pirate Pendant

THIS SKULL AND CROSSBONES PENDANT WILL APPEAL TO ALL WANNABE PIRATES AND MAKES A COOL ACCESSORY THAT COULD BE TRANSFORMED INTO A BADGE OR KEY RING, TOO.

WHAT YOU WILL NEED

- Template on page 79
- Card for template
- Pencil and scissors
- Sheet of black card
- Sheet of black felt
- White/PVA glue
- Sheet of gray felt
- Hole punch
- 24in (60cm) red cord

CUT THE SHAPE Copy the template on page 79 and cut out. Place the template on top of the black card, draw around it with a pencil, and cut out the shape; turn the card not the scissors on the curved shapes.

GLUE THE FELT Put some dabs of glue on your card shape and stick the black felt on top. When the glue has dried cut out around the card shape. Repeat to add a layer of felt to the other side of the card.

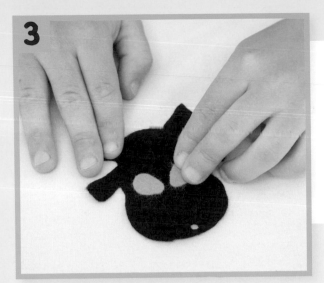

3

ADD THE EYES Use the template to cut two small circles from the gray felt, to make the eyes, and stick to the front of the skull and crossbones with a dab of glue. Make a hole at the top of the skull in the center, with a hole punch.

4

THREAD THE CORD Tie the two ends of the cord together to make a loop. Thread 2in (5cm) of the loop through the hole from back to front. Take the knot through the loop and pull gently to tighten the cord around the pendant.

Crafty Tip

You can make this in lots of different color combinations, or go for classic white skull with black eyes for a spooky effect!

Pine Cone Folk

THESE CUTE LITTLE CHARACTERS ARE BROUGHT TO LIFE WITH SOME FUN CRAFT MATERIALS. GO FOR A WOODLAND WALK TO FIND YOUR PINE CONES AND, ONCE BACK HOME, THERE'S LOTS OF PAINTING AND GLUING FUN TO INVOLVE LITTLE ONES IN CREATING THESE SWEET PLAYMATES.

WHAT YOU WILL NEED

- Pine cones
- Small paintbrush
- White acrylic paint
- Cotton balls
- White/PVA glue
- Googly eyes
- Craft pom-poms for nose
- Template on page 75
- Card for template
- Pencil and scissors
- Felt or fabric for the hat
- Ricrac trim and small buttons, beads, or shapes
- Scraps of felt for scarf and feet

1

PREPARE THE PINE CONE Push the top of the pine cone down on a hard, flat surface to flatten it—if you need to, cut or twist off the tip. This is where the head will go.

PAINT THE SNOW Paint the tips of the pine cone leaves with white paint to give it a snowy effect and set aside to dry.

2

3

ADD THE FACE Take a cotton ball and glue on some googly eyes and a small craft pom-pom for a nose.

CUT OUT FELT HAT Copy the template on page 75 onto card and cut out. Trace around the circle onto a piece of felt and cut it out. Cut the circle in half and then fold the semicircle in half and out again to make a quarter shape.

4

5

MAKE THE HAT Roll the quarter circle of felt into a cone and glue it together along the long side to make a pointy hat. Glue a piece of ricrac trim around the hat to decorate it, and add a little button if you like.

MAKE THE FEET Copy the template on page 75, cut out, and trace around it on felt. Cut out two feet.

MAKE THE SCARF Cut a strip of felt for the scarf, making sure it is long enough to go around the pine cone and overlap a little at the neck.

ASSEMBLE Now it's time to put all the pieces together. Glue the cotton ball head to the pine cone. Wrap the scarf around the neck, and glue the overlapping ends together.

9

ATTACH HAT AND FEET Carefully glue the hat to the head and the feet to the base. Let it dry completely.

Crazy Sock Creature

CHOOSE BRIGHTLY COLORED AND PATTERNED SOCKS TO USE FOR THIS FUN TOY. INVOLVE YOUR CHILD IN THE DESIGN PROCESS—CHOOSING THE BUTTONS AND YARN COLORS—AND HELPING WITH STUFFING AND DECORATING. THEY'LL LOVE WATCHING THE TRANSFORMATION FROM SOCK TO TOY. THIS IS A GOOD PROJECT FOR FIRST SEWING PRACTICE, TOO.

WHAT YOU WILL NEED

- Brightly colored patterned sock without any holes
- Sewing kit
- Contrasting colored embroidery floss/thread
- Cotton balls
- 3 buttons
- Yarn/wool for hair
- Scissors
- White/PVA glue

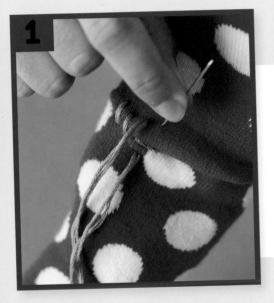

STITCH MOUTH Use your fingers to fold the heel of the sock inward so it forms a mouth shape. Use brightly colored floss/thread to make a feature of the mouth and oversew across the fold of the heel.

STUFF SOCK Use lots of cotton balls to stuff the sock. You may need to use the end of a paintbrush to push the stuffing right to the end. Insert enough stuffing so the toy is plump and easy to hold. When you have finished, oversew the bottom of the sock closed.

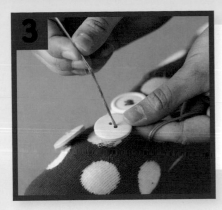

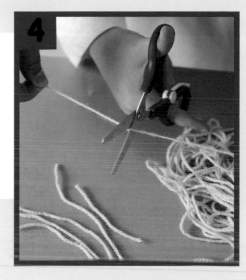

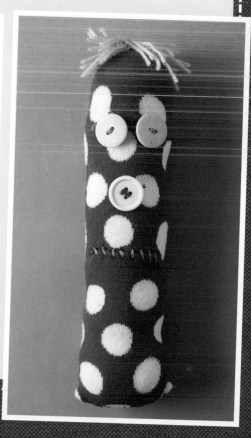

SEW ON BUTTONS Sew on two buttons for the eyes, about 1¼in (3cm) above the heel and roughly ¾in (2cm) apart. Add another button for the nose just below the eyes.

MAKE HAIR Cut about 20 strands of yarn, each measuring about 4in (10cm) long. Use one of the lengths to firmly tie the strands together in the middle.

GLUE HAIR Add a generous dab of glue to the mop of hair and stick it to the top of the sock creature.

Fabric-wrapped Bangle

THIS IS A GREAT PROJECT FOR USING UP LEFTOVER FABRIC SCRAPS OR RECYCLING YOUR CHILD'S FAVORITE OUTGROWN CLOTHES. PRETTY FLORAL PATTERNS OR SMALL DESIGNS WORK REALLY WELL, AND YOU CAN ADD GLITTER AND SPARKLES TO EXTEND THE ACTIVITY FOR THOSE WHO LIKE A LITTLE BLING!

WHAT YOU WILL NEED
- Scissors
- Piece of patterned fabric (at least 24in/60cm long)
- Plastic bangle
- Glue stick or fabric glue

CUT FABRIC STRIP Carefully cut a long strip of fabric, about 24in (60cm) long and 1in (2.5cm) wide.

GLUE TO BANGLE Take the end of your fabric strip and glue it to the inside of your bangle. Let it dry for a few minutes.

Crafty Tip

A slightly frayed edge to the fabric can give the bangles a vintage feel, so you can skip the trimming stage if you wish. Alternatively, you could use pinking shears to cut the length of fabric. This will prevent fraying and also give an interesting crinkly effect.

3

WRAP FABRIC Begin to wrap the fabric strip around the bangle, making sure it overlaps each time and that none of the plastic bangle is showing through. Continue wrapping until the entire bangle is covered with fabric.

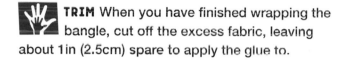

TRIM When you have finished wrapping the bangle, cut off the excess fabric, leaving about 1in (2.5cm) spare to apply the glue to.

4

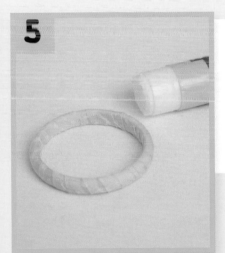

5

GLUE END Apply plenty of glue to the end of the fabric strip and stick it to the inside of the bangle so it is invisible when it is worn. Trim off any stray bits of cotton that may have frayed during the wrapping process.

Spoon Puppets

THIS IS GREAT ACTIVITY FOR A PLAY DATE. SIMPLY DRAW FACES ONTO WOODEN SPOONS, ADD A FETCHING HAIRSTYLE AND SOME SIMPLE CLOTHES, AND THEY ARE READY TO PLAY.

WHAT YOU WILL NEED

- A wooden spoon or spatula
- Felt-tipped pens
- Scraps of fabric
- Fabric scissors or pinking shears (optional)
- Embroidery floss/thread and needle
- White/PVA glue
- Ribbons and buttons, to decorate
- Scraps of yarn/wool

1

DRAW FACE Use felt-tipped pens to draw a face onto the back of the wooden spoon or spatula.

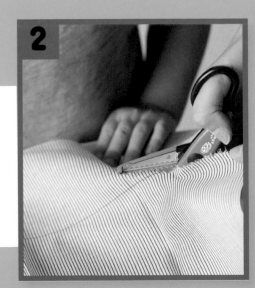

2

MEASURE FABRIC Cut out a piece of fabric measuring about 12 x 5in (30 x 13cm)—if you have pinking shears, use them to give a zig-zag edge and prevent fraying.

3

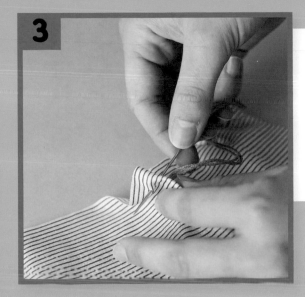

✋ **GATHER FABRIC** Cut a length of embroidery floss/thread and thread the needle. Sew running stitch across the top of the fabric, leaving about 4in (10cm) of floss at each end. Gather up the fabric by pulling the floss.

✋ **TIE ON FABRIC** Position the gathered fabric centered beneath the spoon, tie the floss around the spoon, fastening with a knot or a bow.

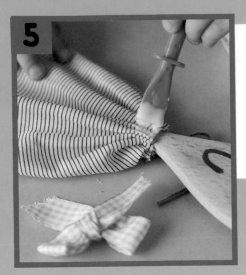

5

DECORATE You can decorate your puppet in a number of ways depending on its character. Glue or tie a ribbon around its neck; or make buttons from felt and glue them onto the fabric. You could also cut out a tie shape in fabric and glue it in place.

ADD HAIR Cut the yarn into lengths to make your puppet's hair. Tie the lengths in the middle and trim them if necessary.

6

7

FINISH Glue the hair to the top of the head. If you like, you could tie a ribbon in the hair or make braids. Let it dry before playing.

Woodland Coasters

A TEA PLAYSET ISN'T REALLY COMPLETE WITHOUT SOME COASTERS. WE'VE MADE OURS FROM FELT CIRCLES AND DECORATED THEM WITH A SQUIRREL AND ACORNS FOR A WOODLAND THEME, BUT YOU COULD USE ANY SHAPES THAT YOU LIKE. REMEMBER TO KEEP ANY DECORATIONS AS FLAT AS POSSIBLE, SO THAT YOUR CUPS WON'T WOBBLE!

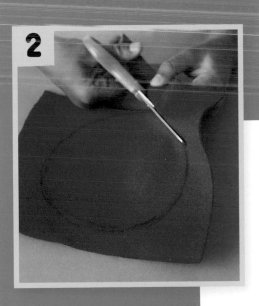

WHAT YOU WILL NEED

- Templates on page 78
- Card for templates
- Pencil and scissors
- Pieces of red, light brown, and ginger felt
- Sheets of colored felt in 2 different colors for each coaster
- White/PVA glue
- Felt-tipped pens
- Stranded embroidery floss/thread and needle
- 3-D fabric paint pens

1 **COPY SHAPES** Copy the templates on page 78 and cut out. Use the templates to cut out a red squirrel, a small ginger acorn, one large light brown acorn cap, and one large ginger acorn. Cut out a small circle for an eye for the squirrel.

CUT OUT COASTERS Cut out two coaster shapes from one shade of green felt and two more from another shade of green. Choose a color for the top of the coasters that the squirrel and acorn colors will stand out against. For the bottom of the coasters, use felt that matches the embroidery floss/thread edging (see Step 6); this makes it easier to hide the finishing stitches.

3

ARRANGE THE SHAPES Put two coaster shapes together and arrange the squirrel and small acorn on top. Put the acorn and acorn cap on the other pair of coasters.

GLUE COASTERS Glue the coaster shapes together with a generous dab of glue, then add the decoration. For the acorn, stick the acorn on first then stick the cap over the top.

4

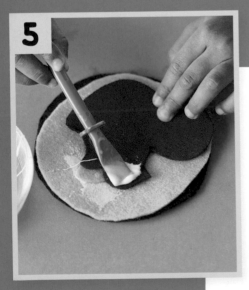

5

GLUE SQUIRREL For the squirrel, glue the small acorn on first, then add the squirrel on top, so that it looks like it is holding the acorn. Finally, glue the eye in place. Using a dark felt-tipped pen, add the pupil in the squirrel's eye.

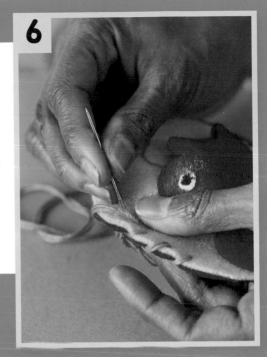

SEW THE COASTERS Cut a length of embroidery floss/thread to contrast with the top of the coasters, separate half the strands (so for six-stranded floss, use three strands), and use a large needle. Use the embroidery floss to oversew the front and back of each coaster together. Hide the knots between the two layers and finish the stitching on the back.

DRAW IN DETAILS Using the dotted lines on the template as reference, draw the leg and the tail on the squirrel, and the lines on the acorn, using a 3-D fabric paint pen. Let dry before using.

Templates

For help on using templates, see page 11.
All the templates are printed at actual size.

Big Flower Brooch
PAGE 30

Finger Puppets
PAGE 28

Sheep's face and ear

Body for lion
and sheep

Lion's mane

Sock Puppet
PAGE 50

Mouth

Eye

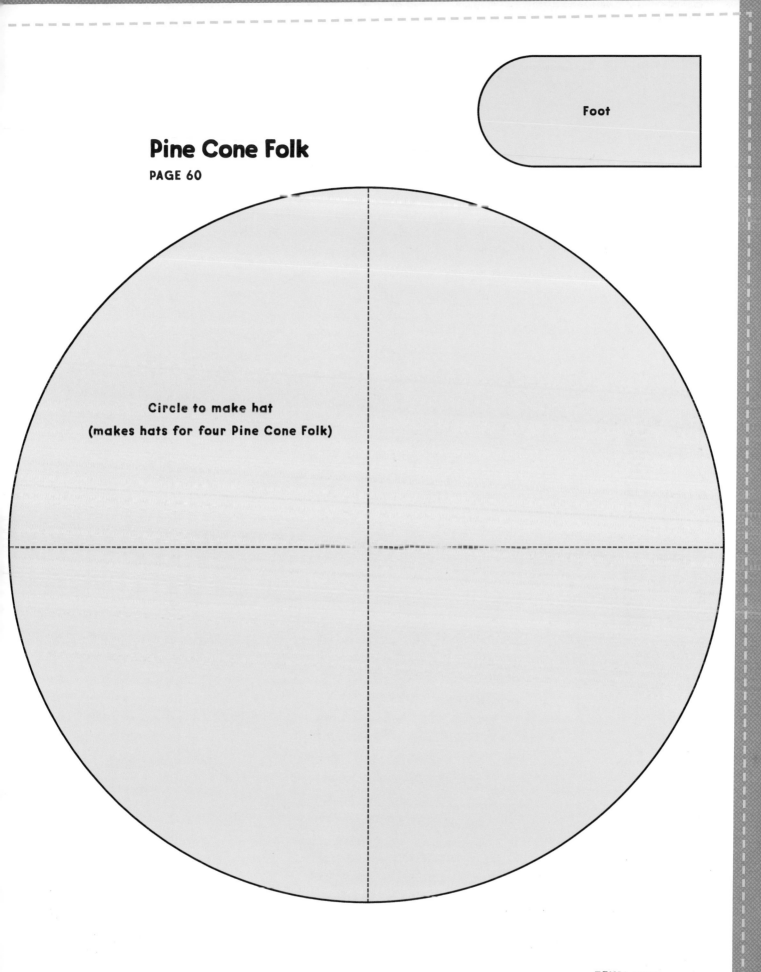

Pine Cone Folk

PAGE 60

Foot

Circle to make hat

(makes hats for four Pine Cone Folk)

Shoebox Jewelry Box
PAGE 21

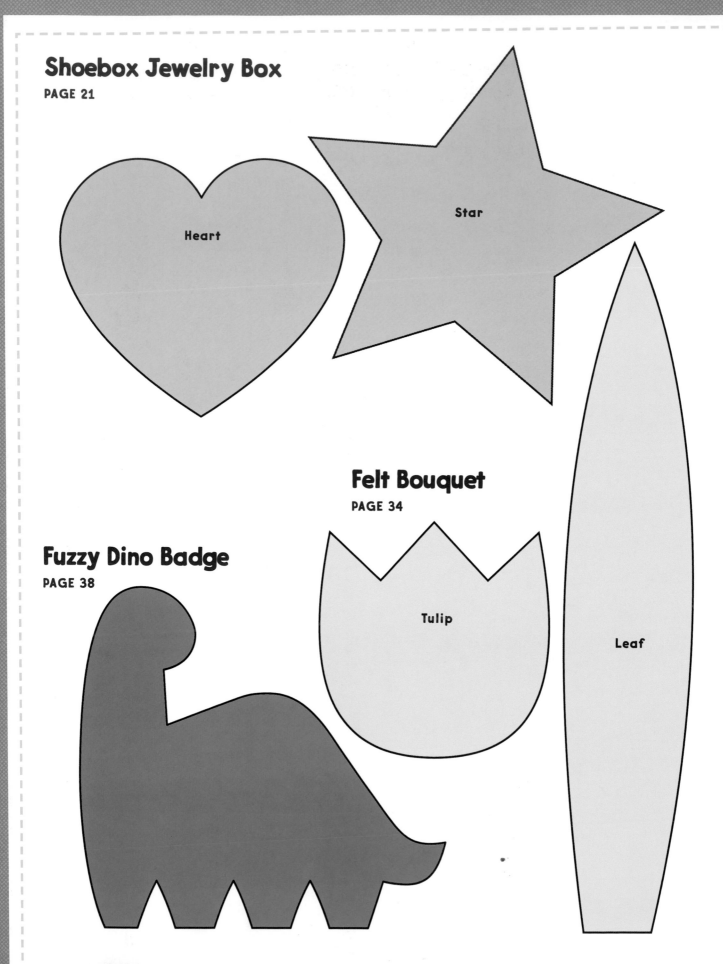

Heart

Star

Felt Bouquet
PAGE 34

Tulip

Leaf

Fuzzy Dino Badge
PAGE 38

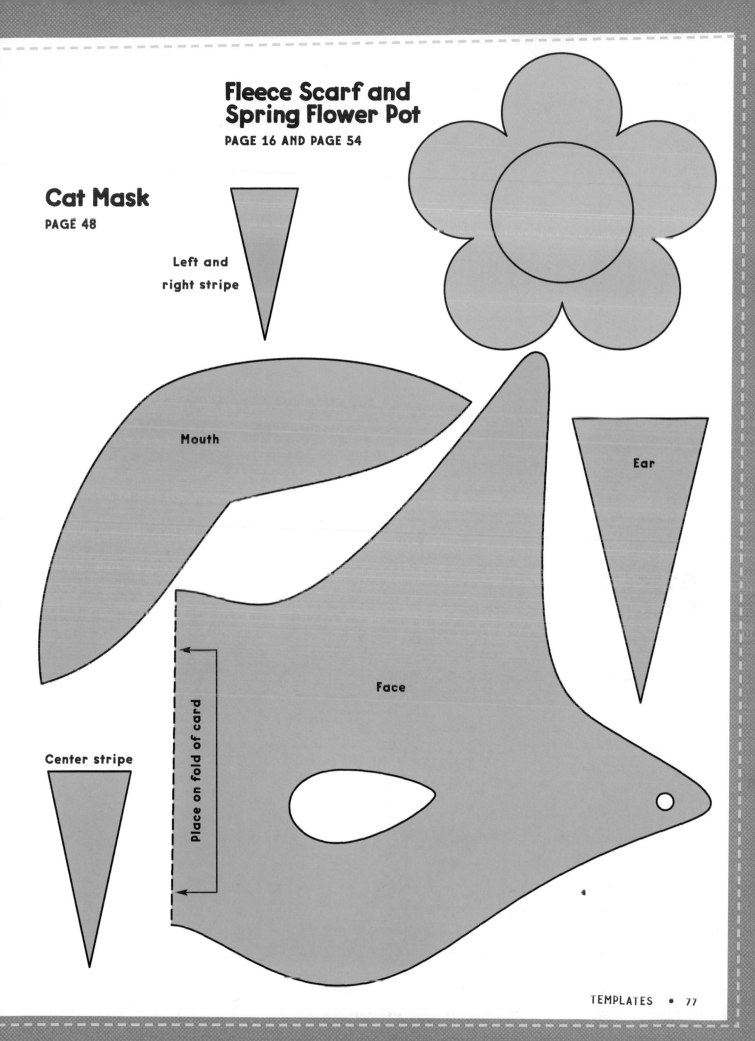

Fleece Scarf and Spring Flower Pot
PAGE 16 AND PAGE 54

Cat Mask
PAGE 48

Left and right stripe

Mouth

Ear

Face

Place on fold of card

Center stripe

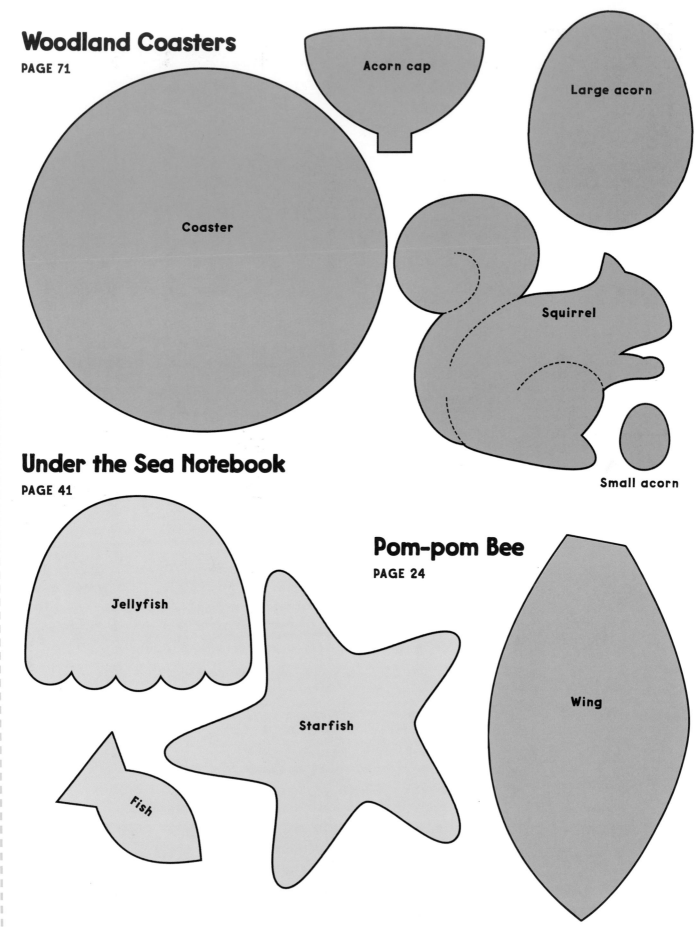

Woodland Coasters
PAGE 71

Acorn cap

Large acorn

Coaster

Squirrel

Small acorn

Under the Sea Notebook
PAGE 41

Jellyfish

Pom-pom Bee
PAGE 24

Starfish

Fish

Wing

Pirate Pendant
PAGE 58

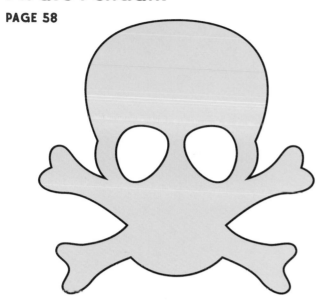

Cotton Ball Sheep
PAGE 46

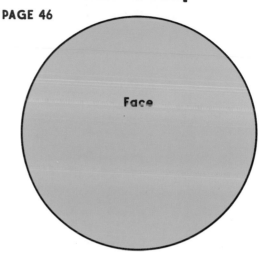

Face

Suppliers

US

A C Moore
www.acmoore.com

Create for Less
www.createforless.com

Creative Kids Crafts
www.creativekidscrafts.com

Darice
www.darice.com

Hobby Lobby
www.hobbylobby.com

Jo-ann Fabric & Crafts
www.joann.com

Michaels
www.michaels.com

Mister Art
www.misterart.com

Walmart
www.walmart.com

UK

Baker Ross
www.bakerross.co.uk

Early Learning Centre
www.elc.co.uk

Hobbycraft
www.hobbycraft.co.uk

Homecrafts Direct
www.homecrafts.co.uk

John Lewis
www.johnlewis.co.uk

Mulberry Bush
www.mulberrybush.co.uk

Paperchase
www.paperchase.co.uk

The Works
www.theworks.co.uk

Yellow Moon
www.yellowmoon.org.uk

Index

CREDITS

Key: T = top, C = center,
B = bottom, L = left, R = right

PROJECT DESIGNERS

Marty Allen: pp. 2BR, 6, 50–51
Libby Abadee and Cath Armstrong:
  pp. 3TL, 34–35
Emily Breen: pp. 24–27, 52–53
Caroline Fernandez: pp. 1, 3BR, 14–15,
  21–23, 46–47, 54–57
Sarah Fiorenza: pp. 2TL, 4C, 5B,
  8T, 12–13, 30–31, 36–40, 44–45,
  58–59, 66–67
Emma Hardy: pp. 2TR, 4B, 8B, 18–20,
  32–33, 68–70
Laura Howard: pp. 4T, 5T, 41–43, 71–73
Mia Underwood: pp. 3BL, 60–63
Catherine Woram: pp. 2BL, 10–11, 16–17,
  28–29, 48–49, 64–65

PHOTOGRAPHERS

Terry Benson: pp. 1–6, 8, 10–13, 16–17,
  24–31, 32TL, 34–43, 44BR, 46–57,
  60–63, 64–65, 68TL, 69CR, 68–73
Martin Norris: pp. 14–15, 21–23
Debbie Patterson: pp. 2TR, 7,
  18–20, 32–33
Penny Wincer: pp. 44–45, 58–59, 66–67
Polly Wreford: p. 31BL

STYLISTS

Emily Breen: pp. 1–6, 8, 10–11, 16–17,
  24–31, 34–43, 46–57, 60–65, 68–73
Emma Hardy: pp. 2TR, 7, 18–20, 32–33
Sophie Martell: pp. 14–15, 21–23
Luis Peral: pp. 12–13, 44–45,
  58–59, 66–67
Catherine Woram: p. 31BL

ILLUSTRATORS

Rachel Boulton: p. 11
Stephen Dew: pp. 6–7